THE PERIODIC TABLE OF ELEMENTS
ALKALI METALS, ALKALINE EARTH METALS AND TRANSITION METALS
CHILDREN'S CHEMISTRY BOOK

BABY PROFESSOR

EDUCATION KIDS

Speedy Publishing LLC
40 E. Main St. #1156
Newark, DE 19711
www.speedypublishing.com
Copyright 2016

Studying and understanding chemistry gives us the amazing opportunity to get into details of how the world around us works. We come to learn that everything in the universe is made up of matter and elements.

Read on and learn amazing facts about the periodic table of elements and the specific details about alkali metals, alkaline Earth Metals, and transition metals!

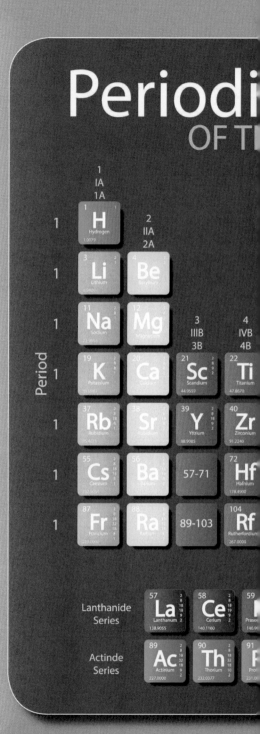

Table
ELEMENTS

Alkali metals
Alkaline earth metals
Lanthanoids
Actinoids
Transition metals

Post-transition
Metalloids
Halogens
Noble gases
Other nonmetals

Atomic number   Per shell

Symbol
Name
Weight

18 VIIIA 8A

13 IIIA 3A	14 IVA 4A	15 VA 5A	16 VIA 6A	17 VIIA 7A	2 **He** Helium 4.0026
5 **B** Boron 10.8100	6 **C** Carbon 12.0110	7 **N** Nitrogen 14.0070	8 **O** Oxygen 15.9990	9 **F** Fluorine 18.9984	10 **Ne** Neon 20.1797
13 **Al** Aluminium 26.9815	14 **Si** Silicon 28.0850	15 **P** Phosphorus 30.9738	16 **S** Sulfur 32.0600	17 **Cl** Chlorine 35.4500	18 **Ar** Argon 39.9480

5 VB 5B	6 VIB 6B	7 VIIB 7B	8 VIII 8	9 VIII	10 VIII	11 IB 1B	12 IIB 2B						
V Vanadium	24 **Cr** Chromium 51.9961	25 **Mn** Manganese 54.9380	26 **Fe** Iron 55.8450	27 **Co** Cobalt 58.9332	28 **Ni** Nickel 58.9634	29 **Cu** Copper 63.5460	30 **Zn** Zinc 65.4090	31 **Ga** Gallium 73.6300	32 **Ge** Germanium 73.6300	33 **As** Arsenic 74.9216	34 **Se** Selenium 78.9600	35 **Br** Bromine 79.9040	36 **Kr** Krypton 83.7980
41 **Nb** Niobium	42 **Mo** Molybdenum 95.9400	43 **Tc** Technetium 98.0000	44 **Ru** Ruthenium 101.0700	45 **Rh** Rhodium 102.9055	46 **Pd** Palladium 106.4200	47 **Ag** Silver 107.8682	48 **Cd** Cadmium 112.4110	49 **In** Indium 114.8180	50 **Sn** Tin 118.7100	51 **Sb** Antimony 121.7600	52 **Te** Tellurium 127.6000	53 **I** Iodine 126.9045	54 **Xe** Xenon 131.2930
Ta Tantalum	**W** Tungsten 183.8400	75 **Re** Rhenium 186.2070	76 **Os** Osmium 190.2300	77 **Ir** Iridium 192.2170	78 **Pt** Platinum 195.0840	79 **Au** Gold 196.9666	80 **Hg** Mercury 200.5900	81 **Tl** Thallium 204.3800	82 **Pb** Lead 207.2000	83 **Bi** Bismuth 208.9804	84 **Po** Polonium 209.0000	85 **At** Astatine 210.0000	86 **Rn** Radon 222.0000
Db Dubnium	106 **Sg** Seaborgium 271.0000	107 **Bh** Bohrium 272.0000	108 **Hs** Hassium 270.0000	109 **Mt** Meitnerium 276.0000	110 **Ds** Darmstadtium 281.0000	111 **Rg** Roentgenium 280.0000	112 **Cn** Copernicium 285.0000	113 **Nh** Nihonium 286.0000	114 **Fl** Flerovium 289.0000	115 **Mc** Moscovium 289.0000	116 **Lv** Livermorium 293.0000	117 **Ts** Tennessine 294.0000	118 **Og** Oganesson 294.0000

60 **Nd** Neodymium 144.2420	61 **Pm** Promethium 145.0000	62 **Sm** Samarium 150.3600	63 **Eu** Europium 151.9640	64 **Gd** Gadolinium 157.2500	65 **Tb** Terbium 158.9253	66 **Dy** Dysprosium 162.5000	67 **Ho** Holmium 164.9303	68 **Er** Erbium 167.2600	69 **Tm** Thulium 168.9342	70 **Yb** Ytterbium 173.0540	71 **Lu** Lutetium 174.9668
92 **U** Uranium 238.0289	93 **Np** Neptunium 237.0000	94 **Pu** Plutonium 244.0000	95 **Am** Americium 243.0000	96 **Cm** Curium 247.0000	97 **Bk** Berkelium 247.0000	98 **Cf** Californium 251.0000	99 **Es** Einsteinium 252.0000	100 **Fm** Fermium 257.0000	101 **Md** Mendelevium 258.0000	102 **No** Nobelium 259.0000	103 **Lr** Lawrencium 262.0000

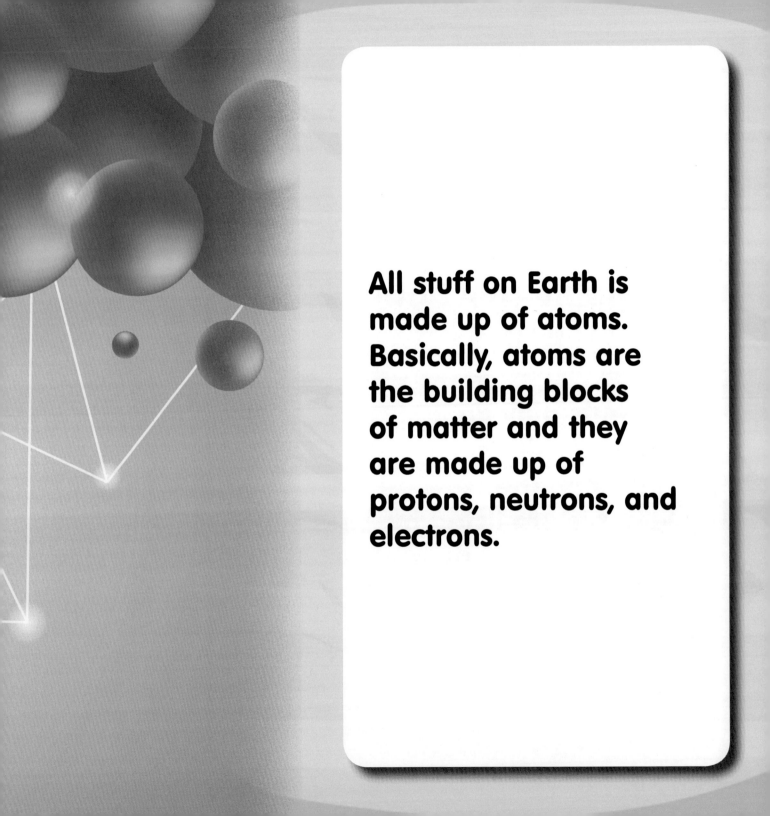

All stuff on Earth is made up of atoms. Basically, atoms are the building blocks of matter and they are made up of protons, neutrons, and electrons.

WHAT IS THE PERIODIC TABLE OF ELEMENTS?

Elements play an amazing role in Chemistry. The elements are listed by the structure of their atoms.

This list is what we call the Periodic Table of Elements. The list of elements includes the number of protons and electrons in their outer shell.

Moreover, the elements in the periodic table are listed according to their atomic number. The atomic number denotes the number of protons in each atom.

97 94

Beryllium

thium

4

3

Be

Li

9.0

6.941

dium

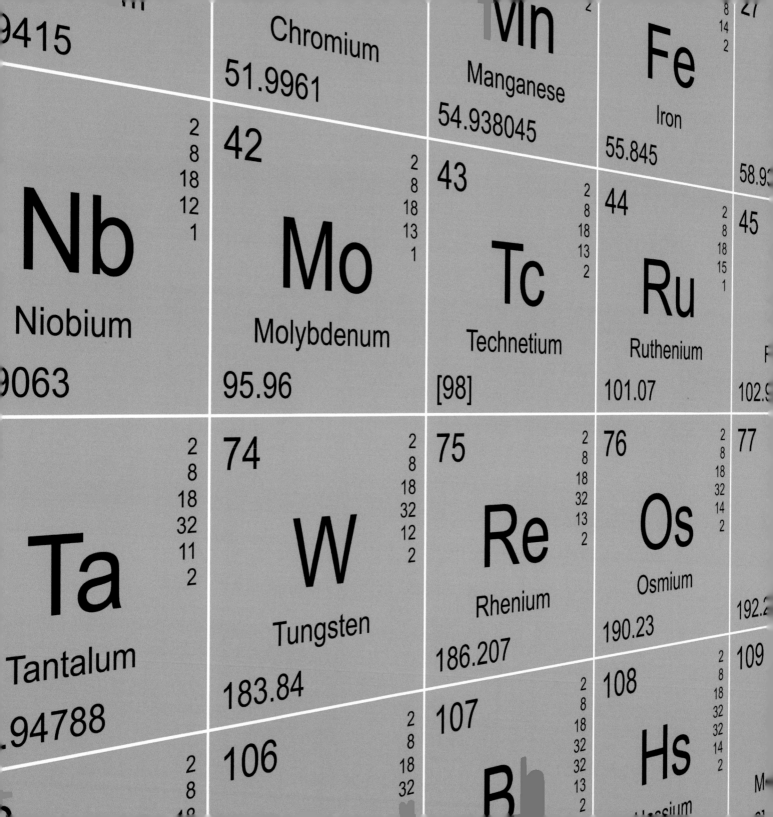

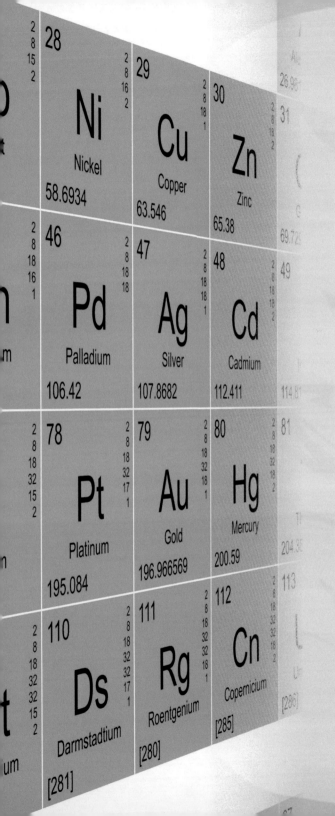

Why is it called Periodic Table of Elements? It is called Periodic Table of Elements because the line-up of elements is in periods or cycles. The period is characterized by the horizontal rows in the table with a total of seven to eight periods.

Elements are lined up in rows, from left to right. The periodic table is the best way to learn elements in Chemistry. This is an impressive guide to learners like you.

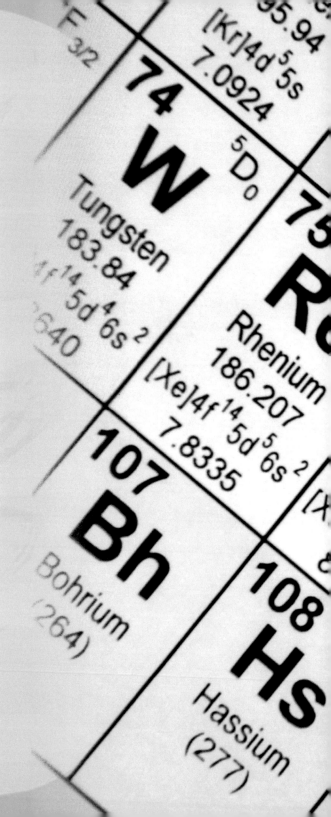

Tc
Technetium
(98)
[Kr]4d⁵ 5s²
7.28

$^6S_{5/2}$

44 Ru
Ruthenium
101.07
[Kr]4d⁷ 5s
7.3605

$^5F_5$

45 Rh
Rhodium
102.90550
[Kr]4d⁸ 5s
7.4589

$^4F_{9/2}$

Iron
55.845
[Ar]3d⁶ 4s²
7.9024

Co
Cobalt
58.933200
[Ar]3d⁷ 4s²
7.8810

$^4F_{9/2}$

Nick
58.693
[Ar]3d⁸ 4s
7.6398

$^6S_{5/2}$

76 Os
Osmium
190.23
[ ]4f¹⁴ 5d⁶ 6s²
382

$^5D_4$

77 Ir
Iridium
192.217
[Xe]4f¹⁴ 5d⁷ 6s²
8.9670

$^4F_{9/2}$

46 Pd
Palladium
106.42
[Kr]4d¹⁰
8.3369

$^1S_0$

78 Pt
Platinum
195.07
[Xe]4f¹⁴

$^3D_3$

Silver
107.868
[Kr]4d¹⁰ 5s
7.5762

79

109
M

WHAT IS AN ELEMENT?

A single type of atom can make up an element. An element is a pure substance. Elements that are joined together become building blocks of matter in the universe.

Examples of elements are Oxygen, Gold, Helium, and Iron. Each element has an important number which is called atomic number. An atomic number is unique in an element.

helium

2

He

4.0026

phosporus

10

Ne

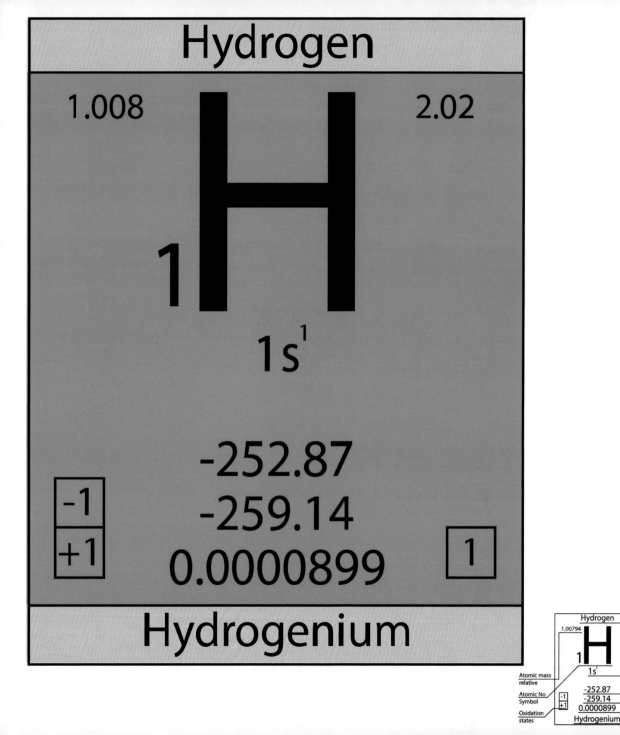

This means that no two elements have the same atomic number. The first element is hydrogen. It consists of only one proton. Therefore, its atomic number is 1.

Let's talk about the spectacular families of elements. Are you ready?

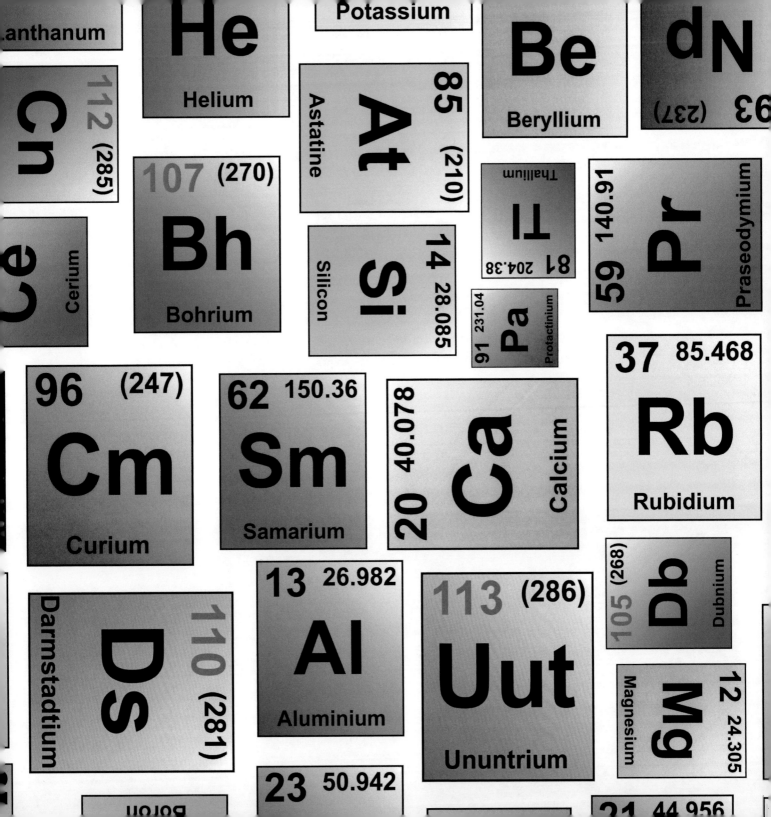

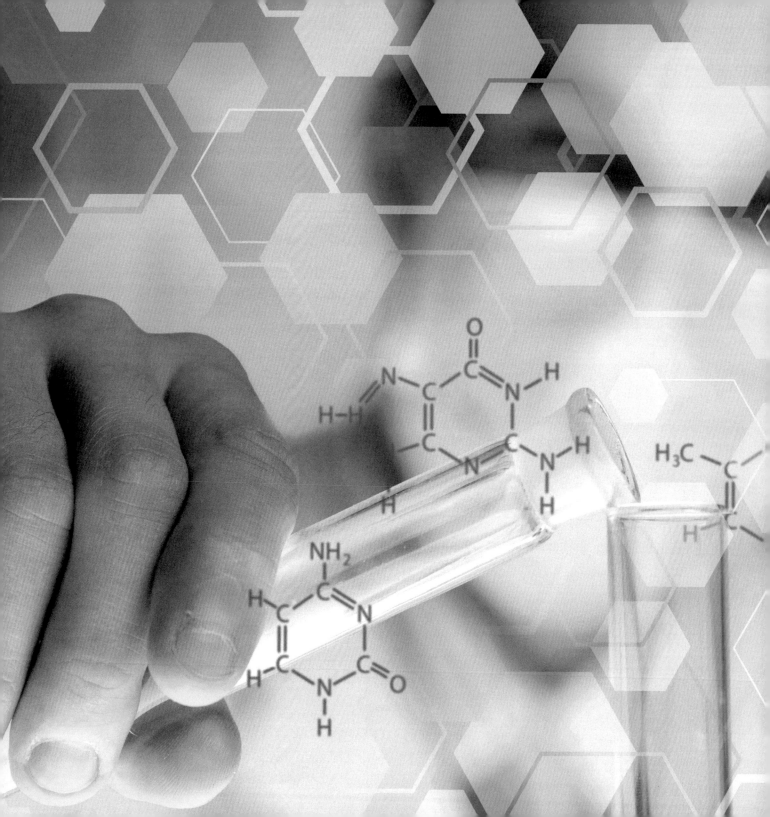

Scientists have discovered a total 118 known elements, of which, 94 elements were believed to be natural and belong to Earth. Some elements have the same properties and they are grouped together, like the following:

ALKALI METALS

These are highly reactive elements in the periodic table. They are also considered as explosive metals. They are found in the first column of the periodic table except hydrogen.

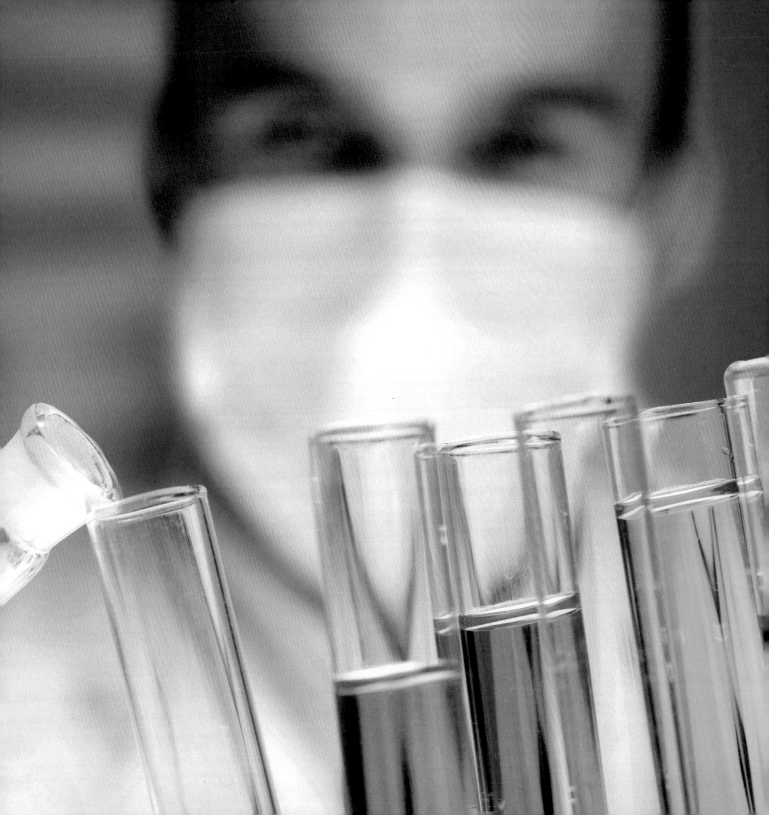

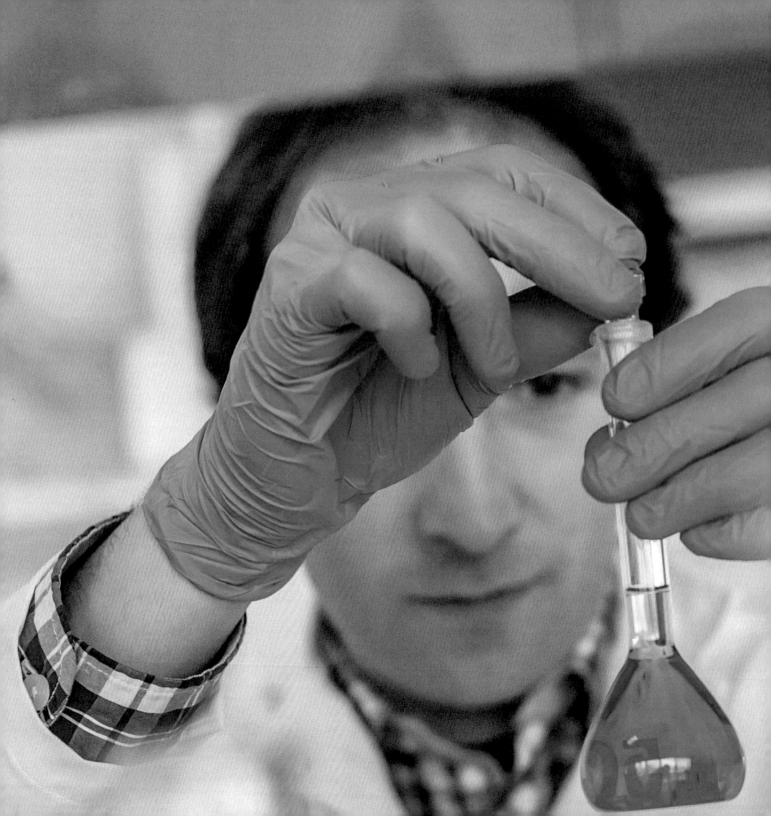

The outer shell of their atom has only one valence electron. The alkali metals and hydrogen are considered as group 1 elements, as shown in the periodic table.

Alkali metals include Potassium, Sodium, Rubidium, Francium, Cesium, and Lithium. Cesium and Francium are considered the most reactive among the alkali metals.

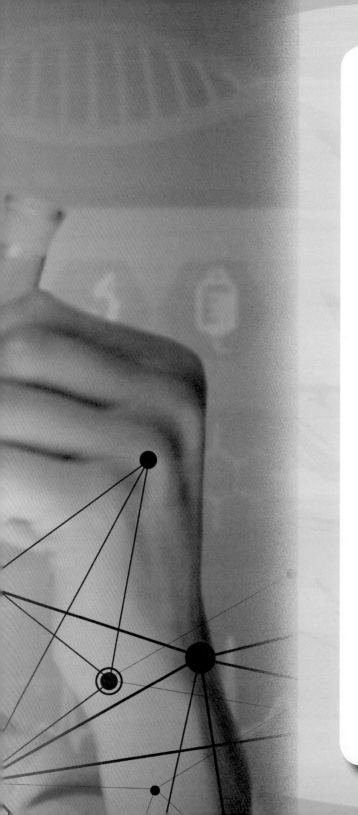

Alkali metals are described to have similar properties. These elements are soft and shiny metals. These soft elements tarnish and react with water when exposed to air.

It is because of oxidation. Alkali metals are good conductors of electricity and heat. They are usually available as salts, not as free elements. Alkali metals are highly reactive with water and air, thus, they are generally stored in oil.

Sodium and Potassium are elements that are considered very important in biological life on the planet. They are very important to life on Earth. The word "alkali" is taken from an Arabic word which means ashes.

When alkali metals are burnt, each of them produce an amazing flame color. Potassium produces lilac-colored flame while Sodium produces orange-colored flame.

4

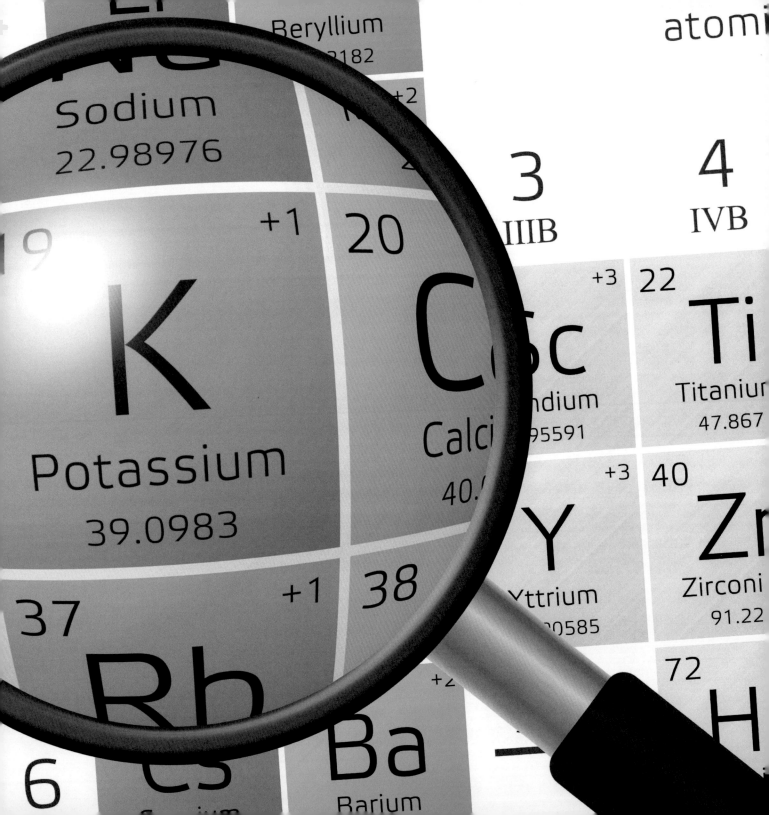

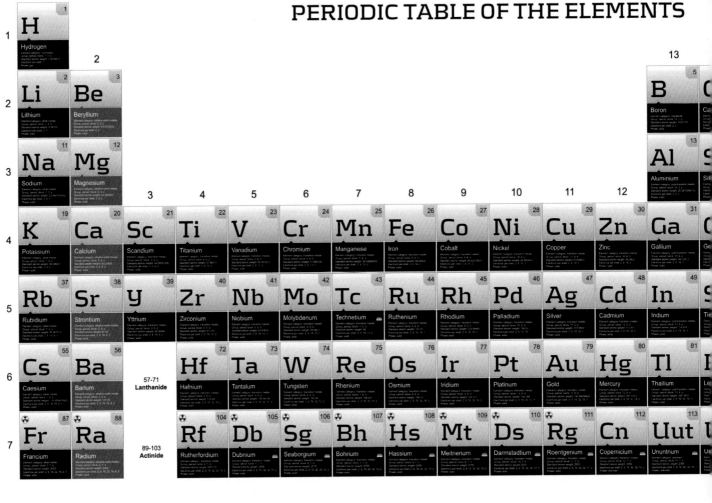

15	16	17	18
			He 2 Helium
N 7 Nitrogen	O 8 Oxygen	F 9 Fluorine	Ne 10 Neon
P 15 Phosphorus	S 16 Sulfur	Cl 17 Chlorine	Ar 18 Argon
As 33 Arsenic	Se 34 Selenium	Br 35 Bromine	Kr 36 Krypton
Sb 51 Antimony	Te 52 Tellurium	I 53 Iodine	Xe 54 Xenon
Bi 83 Bismuth	Po 84 Polonium	At 85 Astatine	Rn 86 Radon
Uup 115 Ununpentium	Uuh 116 Ununhexium	Uus 117 Ununseptium	Uuo 118 Ununoctium

Tm 69 Thulium	Yb 70 Ytterbium	Lu 71 Lutetium
Md 101 Mendelevium	No 102 Nobelium	Lr 103 Lawrencium

ALKALINE EARTH METALS

These belong to group 2 elements in the Periodic Table and are located in the second column. The Alkaline Earth metals are Magnesium, Beryllium, Calcium, Magnesium, Barium, Strontium, and Radium.

These elements are shiny, silvery and soft metals. They are characterized to have two outer valence electrons which are found in compounds and minerals.

vanadium
23
V
50.942

chromium
24
Cr
51.996

Ti
7.867

onium
40
Zr
91.224

niobium
41
Nb
92.906

molybder
42
M
95.

hafnium
72
Hf
178.49

tantalum
73
Ta
180.95

tung

rutherfordium
104
Rf
[261]

dubnium
105
Db
[262]

se

manganese
25
Mn
54.938
iron
26
Fe
55.845
cobalt
27
Co
58.933
nickel
28
Ni
58.693
copper
29
Cu
63.546
zinc
30
Zn
65.38
technetium
43
Tc
[98]
ruthenium
Ru
101.07
rhodium
45
Rh
102.91
palladium
46
Pd
106.42
silver
47
Ag
107.87
cadmium
48
Cd
112.41
rhenium
75
Re
186.21
osmium
76
Os
190.23
iridium
77
Ir
192.22
platinum
78
Pt
195.08
gold
79
Au
196.97
mercury
80
Hg
200.59
bohrium
107
Bh
[264]
hassium
108
Hs
[277]
Mt
[268]
darmstadtium
110
Ds
[271]
roentgenium
111
Rg
[272]
samarium
europium
63
gadolinium
64

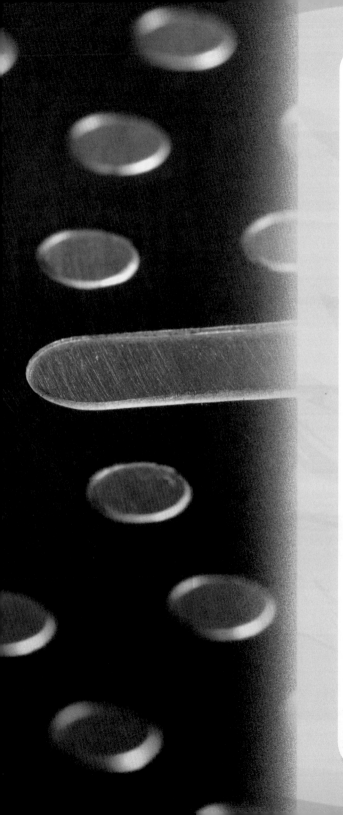

These metals take place in nature and are reactive on certain conditions. They react with water except Beryllium. Calcium is the most abundant Alkaline Earth Metal.

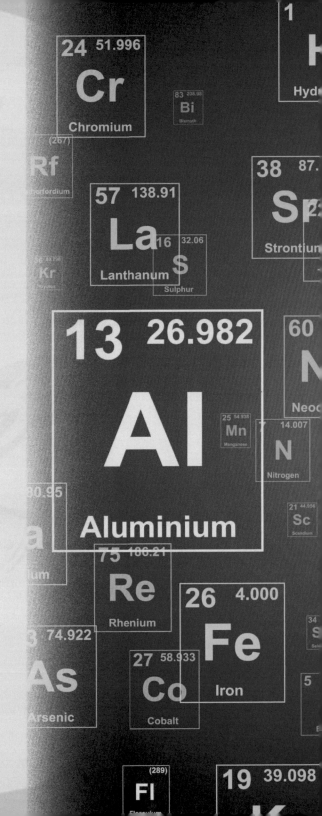

Calcium and Magnesium are two very important elements for animal and plant life. Calcium, for example, is highly needed to build strong bones and regulate our body's temperature.

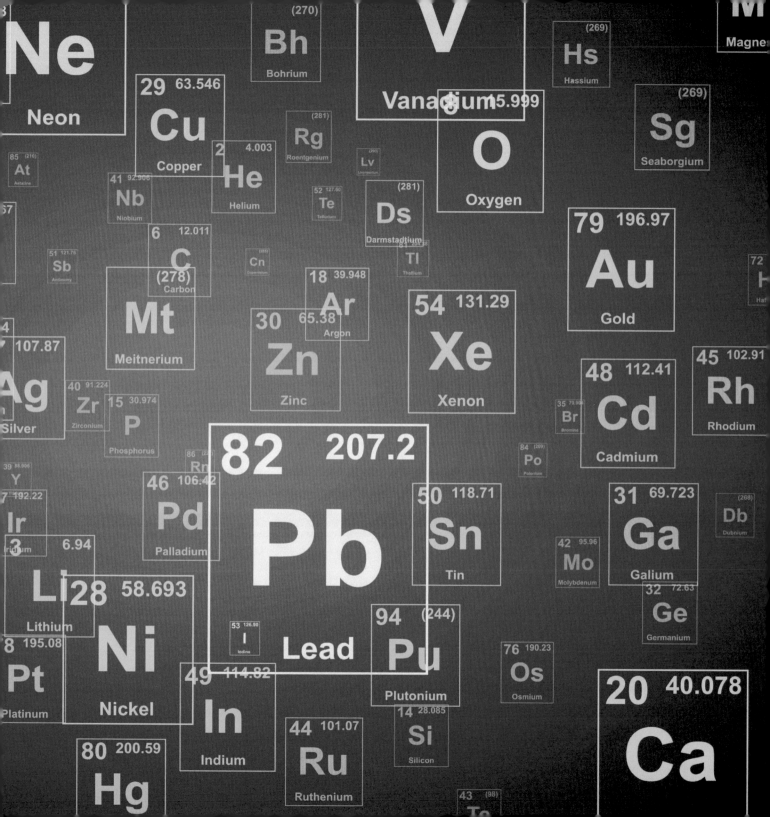

TRANSITION METALS
PERIODIC TABLE OF THE ELEMENTS

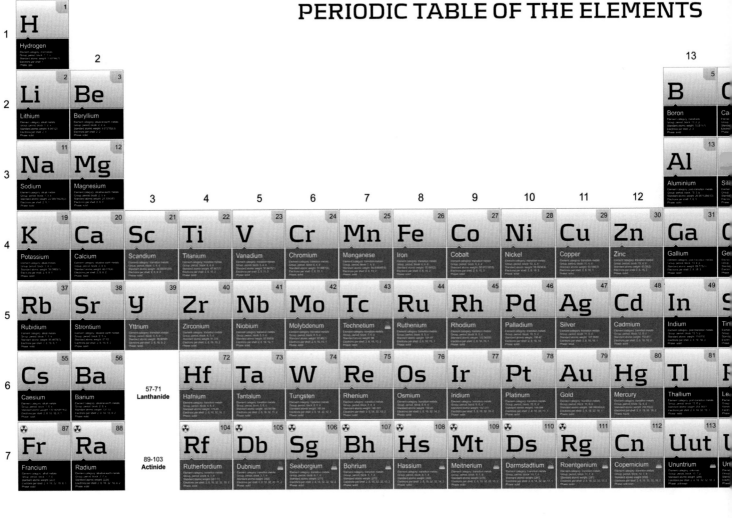

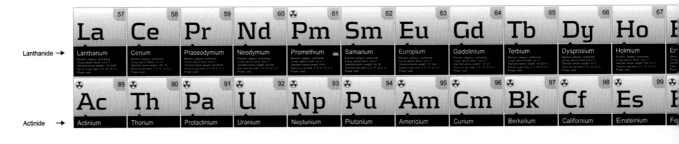

			18
			2 He Helium

15	16	17	
7 N Nitrogen	**8** O Oxygen	**9** F Fluorine	**10** Ne Neon
15 P Phosphorus	**16** S Sulfur	**17** Cl Chlorine	**18** Ar Argon
33 As Arsenic	**34** Se Selenium	**35** Br Bromine	**36** Kr Krypton
51 Sb Antimony	**52** Te Tellurium	**53** I Iodine	**54** Xe Xenon
83 Bi Bismuth	**84** Po Polonium	**85** At Astatine	**86** Rn Radon
115 Uup Ununpentium	**116** Uuh Ununhexium	**117** Uus Ununseptium	**118** Uuo Ununoctium

69	70	71
69 Tm Thulium	**70** Yb Ytterbium	**71** Lu Lutetium
101 Md Mendelevium	**102** No Nobelium	**103** Lr Lawrencium

TRANSITION METALS

The following are examples of transition metals in the periodic table of elements: Titanium, Copper, Nickel, Silver, Platinum, and Gold. They are referred to as the "d-block" which has 35 total elements.

They are considered as Group 3 elements in the Periodic Table. These elements are found at the center of the Periodic Table occupying the principal section including columns 3 through 12.

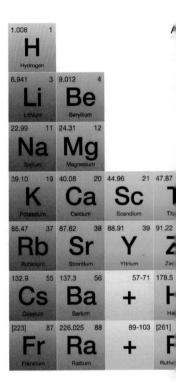

Lanthanide +

Actinide +

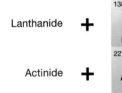

ϽIC TABLE OF THE ELEMENTS

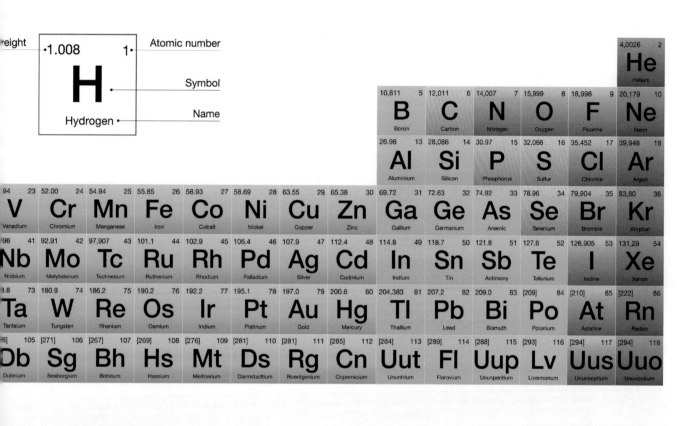

Legend box:
- eight / Atomic number
- 1.008 | 1 — Atomic number
- **H** — Symbol
- Hydrogen — Name

						4.0026 2
						He Helium

10.811 5	12.011 6	14.007 7	15.999 8	18.998 9	20.179 10
B Boron	**C** Carbon	**N** Nitrogen	**O** Oxygen	**F** Fluorine	**Ne** Neon

26.98 13	28.086 14	30.97 15	32.066 16	35.452 17	39.948 18
Al Aluminium	**Si** Silicon	**P** Phosphorus	**S** Sulfur	**Cl** Chlorine	**Ar** Argon

.94 23	52.00 24	54.94 25	55.85 26	58.93 27	58.69 28	63.55 29	65.38 30	69.72 31	72.63 32	74.92 33	78.96 34	79.904 35	83.80 36
V Vanadium	**Cr** Chromium	**Mn** Manganese	**Fe** Iron	**Co** Cobalt	**Ni** Nickel	**Cu** Copper	**Zn** Zinc	**Ga** Gallium	**Ge** Germanium	**As** Arsenic	**Se** Selenium	**Br** Bromine	**Kr** Krypton

.96 41	92.91 42	97.907 43	101.1 44	102.9 45	106.4 46	107.9 47	112.4 48	114.8 49	118.7 50	121.8 51	127.6 52	126.905 53	131.29 54
Nb Niobium	**Mo** Molybdenum	**Tc** Technetium	**Ru** Ruthenium	**Rh** Rhodium	**Pd** Palladium	**Ag** Silver	**Cd** Cadmium	**In** Indium	**Sn** Tin	**Sb** Antimony	**Te** Tellurium	**I** Iodine	**Xe** Xenon

3.8 73	180.9 74	186.2 75	190.2 76	192.2 77	195.1 78	197.0 79	200.6 80	204.383 81	207.2 82	209.0 83	[209] 84	[210] 85	[222] 86
Ta Tantalum	**W** Tungsten	**Re** Rhenium	**Os** Osmium	**Ir** Iridium	**Pt** Platinum	**Au** Gold	**Hg** Mercury	**Tl** Thallium	**Pb** Lead	**Bi** Bismuth	**Po** Polonium	**At** Astatine	**Rn** Radon

8] 105	[271] 106	[267] 107	[269] 108	[276] 109	[281] 110	[281] 111	[285] 112	[284] 113	[289] 114	[288] 115	[293] 116	[294] 117	[294] 118
Db Dubnium	**Sg** Seaborgium	**Bh** Bohrium	**Hs** Hassium	**Mt** Meitnerium	**Ds** Darmstadtium	**Rg** Roentgenium	**Cn** Copernicium	**Uut** Ununtrium	**Fl** Flerovium	**Uup** Ununpentium	**Lv** Livermorium	**Uus** Ununseptium	**Uuo** Ununoctium

.115 58	140.908 59	144.24 60	144.913 61	150.36 62	151.965 63	157.25 64	158.925 65	162.50 66	164.93 67	167.26 68	168.934 69	173.04 70	174.967 71
Ce Cerium	**Pr** Praseodymium	**Nd** Neodymium	**Pm** Promethium	**Sm** Samarium	**Eu** Europium	**Gd** Gadolinium	**Tb** Terbium	**Dy** Dysprosium	**Ho** Holmium	**Er** Erbium	**Tm** Thulium	**Yb** Ytterbium	**Lu** Lutetium

.038 90	231.036 91	238.029 92	237.048 93	244.064 94	243.061 95	247.07 96	247.07 97	251.08 98	252.083 99	257.095 100	258.1 101	259.1 102	262.11 103
h Thorium	**Pa** Protactinium	**U** Uranium	**Np** Neptunium	**Pu** Plutonium	**Am** Americium	**Cm** Curium	**Bk** Berkelium	**Cf** Californium	**Es** Einsteinium	**Fm** Fermium	**Md** Mendelevium	**No** Nobelium	**Lr** Lawrencium

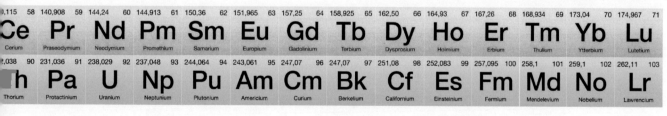

Alkaline earth metal	Transition metal	Post-transition metal	Metalloid	Polyatomic nonmetal	Diatomic nonmetal	Noble gas

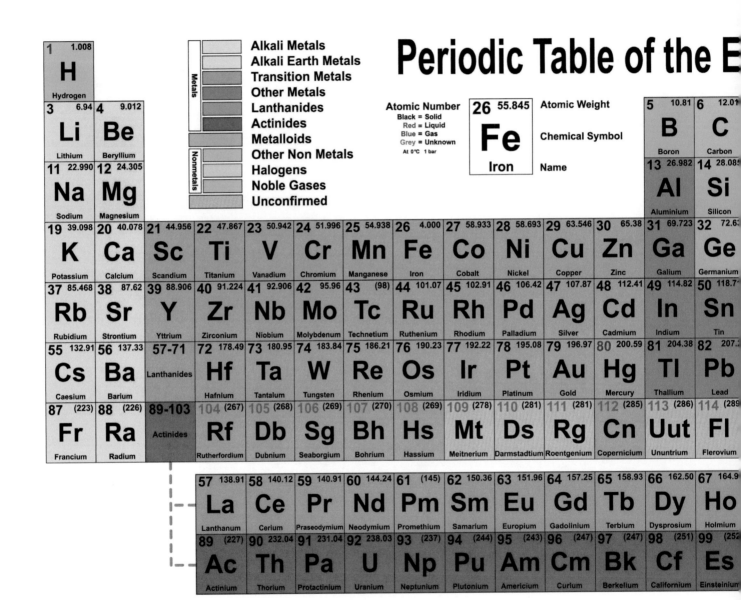

Periodic Table of the E

Alkali Metals
Alkali Earth Metals
Transition Metals
Other Metals
Lanthanides
Actinides
Metalloids
Other Non Metals
Halogens
Noble Gases
Unconfirmed

Metals
Nonmetals

Atomic Number
Black = Solid
Red = Liquid
Blue = Gas
Grey = Unknown
At 0°C 1 bar

26	55.845	Atomic Weight
Fe		Chemical Symbol
Iron		Name

1	1.008
H	
Hydrogen	

3	6.94	4	9.012
Li		**Be**	
Lithium		Beryllium	

11	22.990	12	24.305
Na		**Mg**	
Sodium		Magnesium	

19	39.098	20	40.078	21	44.956	22	47.867	23	50.942	24	51.996	25	54.938	26	4.000	27	58.933	28	58.693	29	63.546	30	65.38
K		**Ca**		**Sc**		**Ti**		**V**		**Cr**		**Mn**		**Fe**		**Co**		**Ni**		**Cu**		**Zn**	
Potassium		Calcium		Scandium		Titanium		Vanadium		Chromium		Manganese		Iron		Cobalt		Nickel		Copper		Zinc	

5	10.81	6	12.01
B		**C**	
Boron		Carbon	

13	26.982	14	28.085
Al		**Si**	
Aluminium		Silicon	

31	69.723	32	72.63
Ga		**Ge**	
Galium		Germanium	

37	85.468	38	87.62	39	88.906	40	91.224	41	92.906	42	95.96	43	(98)	44	101.07	45	102.91	46	106.42	47	107.87	48	112.41	49	114.82	50	118.7
Rb		**Sr**		**Y**		**Zr**		**Nb**		**Mo**		**Tc**		**Ru**		**Rh**		**Pd**		**Ag**		**Cd**		**In**		**Sn**	
Rubidium		Strontium		Yttrium		Zirconium		Niobium		Molybdenum		Technetium		Ruthenium		Rhodium		Palladium		Silver		Cadmium		Indium		Tin	

55	132.91	56	137.33	57-71		72	178.49	73	180.95	74	183.84	75	186.21	76	190.23	77	192.22	78	195.08	79	196.97	80	200.59	81	204.38	82	207.2
Cs		**Ba**		Lanthanides		**Hf**		**Ta**		**W**		**Re**		**Os**		**Ir**		**Pt**		**Au**		**Hg**		**Tl**		**Pb**	
Caesium		Barium				Hafnium		Tantalum		Tungsten		Rhenium		Osmium		Iridium		Platinum		Gold		Mercury		Thallium		Lead	

87	(223)	88	(226)	89-103		104	(267)	105	(268)	106	(269)	107	(270)	108	(269)	109	(278)	110	(281)	111	(281)	112	(285)	113	(286)	114	(289
Fr		**Ra**		Actinides		**Rf**		**Db**		**Sg**		**Bh**		**Hs**		**Mt**		**Ds**		**Rg**		**Cn**		**Uut**		**Fl**	
Francium		Radium				Rutherfordium		Dubnium		Seaborgium		Bohrium		Hassium		Meitnerium		Darmstadtium		Roentgenium		Copernicium		Ununtrium		Flerovium	

57	138.91	58	140.12	59	140.91	60	144.24	61	(145)	62	150.36	63	151.96	64	157.25	65	158.93	66	162.50	67	164.9
La		**Ce**		**Pr**		**Nd**		**Pm**		**Sm**		**Eu**		**Gd**		**Tb**		**Dy**		**Ho**	
Lanthanum		Cerium		Praseodymium		Neodymium		Promethium		Samarium		Europium		Gadolinium		Terbium		Dysprosium		Holmium	

89	(227)	90	232.04	91	231.04	92	238.03	93	(237)	94	(244)	95	(243)	96	(247)	97	(247)	98	(251)	99	(252
Ac		**Th**		**Pa**		**U**		**Np**		**Pu**		**Am**		**Cm**		**Bk**		**Cf**		**Es**	
Actinium		Thorium		Protactinium		Uranium		Neptunium		Plutonium		Americium		Curium		Berkelium		Californium		Einsteinium	

		2 4.003 **He** Helium
nents		
007 8 15.999 **O** Oxygen	9 18.998 **F** Flourine	10 20.180 **Ne** Neon
•74 16 32.06 **S** Sulphur	17 35.453 **Cl** Chlorine	18 39.948 **Ar** Argon
•22 34 78.96 **Se** Selenium	35 79.904 **Br** Bromine	36 83.798 **Kr** Krypton
.76 52 127.60 **Te** Tellurium	53 126.90 **I** Iodine	54 131.29 **Xe** Xenon
.98 84 (209) **Po** Polonium	85 (210) **At** Astatine	86 (222) **Rn** Radon
38) 116 (293) **Lv** Livermorium	117 (294) **Uus** Ununseptium	118 (294) **Uuo** Ununoctium

26 69 168.93 **Tm** Thulium	70 173.05 **Yb** Ytterbium	71 174.97 **Lu** Lutetium
57) (258) **Md** Mendelevium	(259) **No** Nobelium	(262) **Lr** Lawrencium

This is how these elements occupy space in the periodic table although the elements in column twelve are occasionally taken as not part of the transition metals like Mercury and Zinc.

Chemists use the "d electron count instead of using valence electrons to describe transition elements. The transition metals are frequently used in different industries because of their unique qualities.

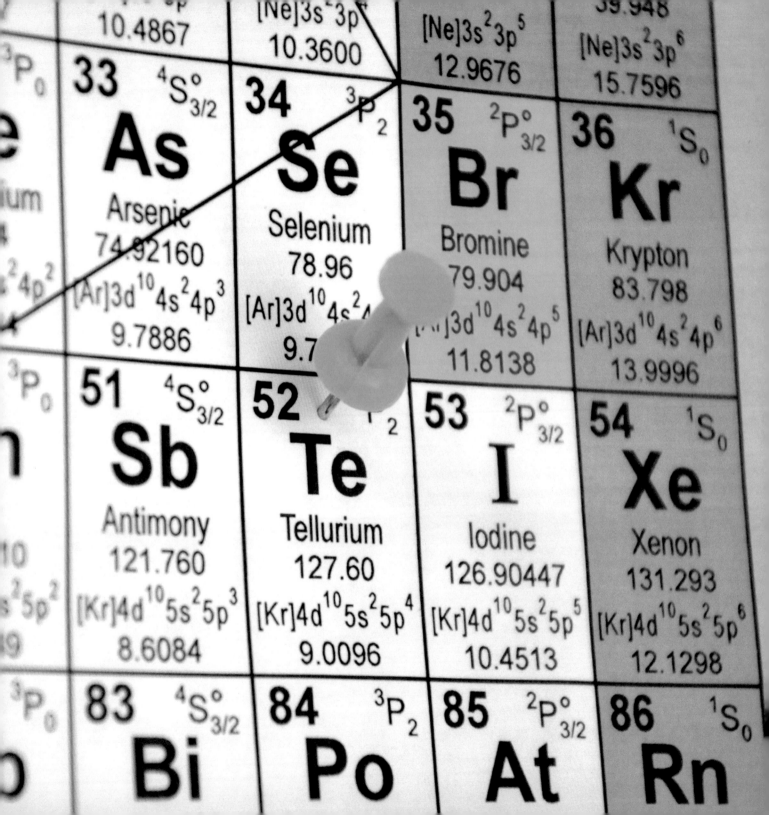

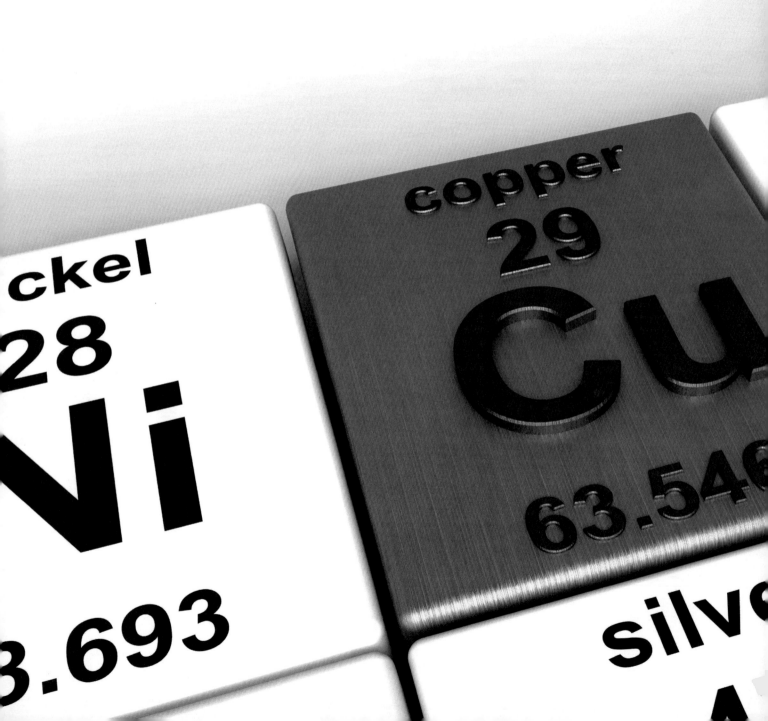

ckel
28
Ni
3.693

copper
29
Cu
63.546

silve

The elements Lanthanides and Actinides are sometimes referred to as transition metals. They are also called inner transition metals. Aside from its outer shell, these elements have incomplete inner subshell.

Transition metals share the same properties like their ability to form compounds with varied colors. They are also conductors of electricity and are paramagnetic. They have high melting and boiling points.

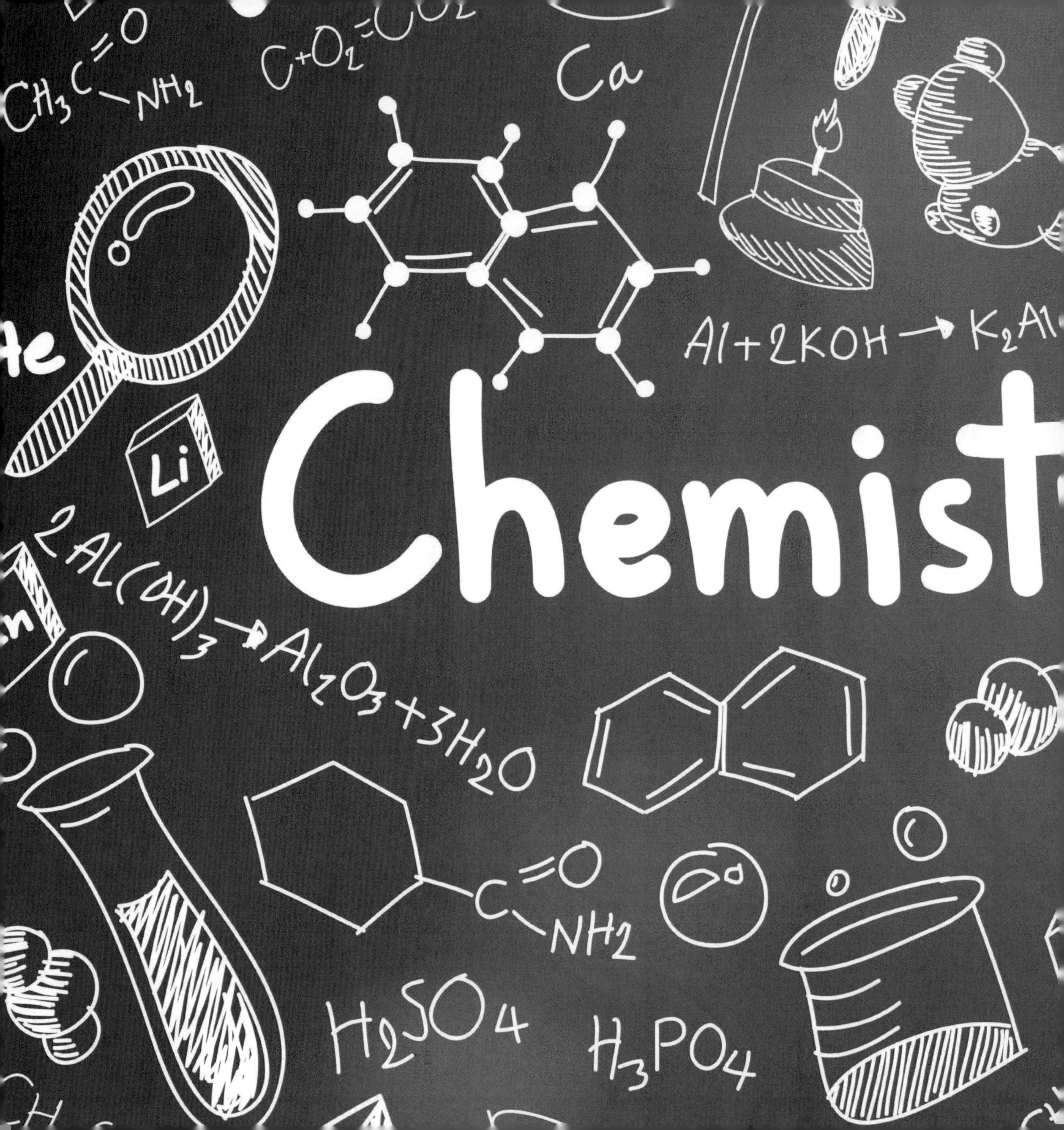

CH_3C=O
NH_2
Ca
Al+2KOH →
Chemist
Li
$2AL(OH)_3 \rightarrow Al_2O_3+3H_2O$
C=O
NH_2
H_2SO_4
H_3PO_4

The mystery around us has been unfolded before our very eyes through the study of Chemistry. Isn't it wonderful to know how the world works and what it is made of? Chemistry is indeed the study of life and truly interesting to discover.

Made in the USA
Lexington, KY
20 November 2017